W9-BON-336

A Note from
Mary Pope Osborne About the

MAGIC
TREE HOUSE®
FACT TRACKERS

When I write Magic Tree House® adventures, I love including facts about the times and places Jack and Annie visit. But when readers finish these adventures, I want them to learn even more. So that's why we write a series of nonfiction books that are companions to the fiction titles in the Magic Tree House® series. We call these books Fact Trackers because we love to track the facts! Whether we're researching dinosaurs, pyramids, Pilgrims, sea monsters, or cobras, we're always amazed at how wondrous and surprising the real world is. We want you to experience the same wonder we do—so get out your pencils and notebooks and hit the trail with us. You can be a Magic Tree House® Fact Tracker, too!

Here's what kids, parents, and teachers have to say about the Magic Tree House® Fact Trackers:

"They are so good. I can't wait for the next one. All I can say for now is prepare to be amazed!" —Alexander N.

"I have read every Magic Tree House book there is. The [Fact Trackers] are a thrilling way to get more information about the special events in the story." —John R.

"These are fascinating nonfiction books that enhance the magical time-traveling adventures of Jack and Annie. I love these books, especially *American Revolution*. I was learning so much, and I didn't even know it!" —Tori Beth S.

"[They] are an excellent 'behind-the-scenes' look at what the [Magic Tree House fiction] has started in your imagination! You can't buy one without the other; they are such a complement to one another." —Erika N., mom

"Magic Tree House [Fact Trackers] took my children on a journey from Frog Creek, Pennsylvania, to so many significant historical events! The detailed manuals are a remarkable addition to the classic fiction Magic Tree House books we adore!" —Jenny S., mom

"[They] are very useful tools in my classroom, as they allow for students to be part of the planning process. Together, we find facts in the [Fact Trackers] to extend the learning introduced in the fictional companions. Researching and planning classroom activities, such as our class Olympics based on facts found in *Ancient Greece and the Olympics*, help create a genuine love for learning!" —Paula H., teacher

MAGIC TREE HOUSE® FACT TRACKER

Benjamin Franklin

A NONFICTION COMPANION TO MAGIC TREE HOUSE #32:
To the Future, Ben Franklin!

BY MARY POPE OSBORNE
AND NATALIE POPE BOYCE

ILLUSTRATED BY ISIDRE MONÉS

A STEPPING STONE BOOK™

Random House 🏠 New York

The Magic Tree House Fact Tracker series was formerly known as the Magic
Tree House Research Guide series.

Visit us on the Web!
MagicTreeHouse.com
rhcbooks.com

Educators and librarians, for a variety of teaching tools, visit us at
RHTeachersLibrarians.com

Library of Congress Cataloging-in-Publication Data
Names: Osborne, Mary Pope, author. | Boyce, Natalie Pope, author. | Monés,
Isidre, illustrator. | Osborne, Mary Pope. To the future, Ben Franklin!
Title: Benjamin Franklin: a nonfiction companion to Magic Tree House #32,
To the future, Ben Franklin / by Mary Pope Osborne and Natalie Pope Boyce;
illustrated by Isidre Monés.
Description: New York: Random House, 2019. | Series: A stepping stone book;
41 | "Magic Tree House Fact Tracker."
Identifiers: LCCN 2018042250 | ISBN 978-1-9848-9317-8 (trade pbk.) |
ISBN 978-1-9848-9318-5 (hardcover library binding) |
ISBN 978-1-9848-9319-2 (ebook)
Subjects: LCSH: Franklin, Benjamin, 1706–1790—Juvenile literature. |
Statesmen—United States—Biography—Juvenile literature. | Inventors—
United States—Biography—Juvenile literature. | Scientists—United States—
Biography—Juvenile literature. | Printers—United States—Biography—
Juvenile literature.
Classification: LCC E302.6.F8 O77 2019 | DDC 973.3092 [B]—dc23

Printed in the United States of America

10 9 8 7 6 5 4 3 2 1

This book has been officially leveled by using the F&P Text Level Gradient™
Leveling System.

For Mary Wilson Taylor and in memory of
The Very Reverend Walter Hamilton Taylor

Historical Consultant:

GEORGE BOUDREAU, PhD, senior research associate, McNeil Center for
Early American Studies, University of Pennsylvania, Philadelphia

With thanks to Karie Diethorn and Dr. Emily Murphy, National Park Serivce

Education Consultant:

HEIDI JOHNSON, language acquisition and science education specialist,
Bisbee, Arizona

Special thanks to the Random House team: Mallory Loehr, Jenna Lettice,
Isidre Monés, Paula Sadler, Jason Zamajtuk, and especially to our beloved
editor, Diane Landolf

Benjamin Franklin

Contents

Dear Readers,

In <u>To the Future, Ben Franklin!</u> we met Benjamin Franklin, one of the greatest Americans in history. He lived 300 years ago, and during our time together, we helped him decide to sign the Constitution of the United States! He was such a big part of the American Revolution that we call him a Founding Father. But Benjamin was also a great inventor, writer, and scientist. He did so many things in his long life that we had to learn more about him.

We read about Benjamin's experiments, especially the one he did

in a terrible thunderstorm with a kite! We also learned that he was a poor boy with only two years of school. In spite of this, Benjamin became famous all over the world. He was the guest of the king of France and one of George Washington's best friends.

So pretend it's the 1700s, and let's travel back in time to get to know all about Benjamin Franklin and his exciting world.

Jack

Annie

1

Benjamin Franklin

Benjamin Franklin was born more than three hundred years ago. Today he is still one of the most famous and beloved men in American history. Benjamin was a great scientist, thinker, inventor, writer, and printer. He created or helped create the first lending library, the first fire department, the first public hospital, and the first post office in America.

When he wasn't working, Benjamin used his spare time wisely. He played music and taught himself five languages. He also learned to swim, and many years after he died, he was made a member of the International Swimming Hall of Fame!

Although people today think of him as <u>Ben</u>, he did not use that nickname.

But Benjamin is probably best known as one of America's Founding Fathers. His wisdom helped guide the country in

its struggle to break free from English rule and become a new nation.

People often wonder how this poor boy, with just two years of school, was able to lead such an amazing life. Benjamin Franklin's story is hard to believe.

Boston

Benjamin was born in Boston, Massachusetts, in 1706. At the time of his birth, the United States wasn't a country. It was divided into thirteen colonies and ruled by England, a country thousands of miles across the ocean.

Boston was part of the Massachusetts Bay Colony. Because the city is on the Atlantic Ocean and has a deep harbor, it was one of the busiest seaports in the colonies.

The Franklin Family

Before Benjamin was born, his father, Josiah, had sailed from England to make a new life in Boston. He owned a shop that sold candles and soap that were

People in the colonies were English subjects with strong ties to Great Britain.

This drawing shows what the Franklin house looked like before it burned in 1810.

made there. Josiah had seven children with his first wife, who later died. He had ten more with his second wife, including Benjamin.

Ben was the fifteenth child and the youngest son. People knew Josiah as a wise man who could be counted on to give good advice.

Josiah worked hard to feed seventeen children!

17

The Franklins lived in a small house with four rooms.

Only about six of Benjamin's brothers and sisters still lived at home when he was a boy.

As a boy, Benjamin taught himself to swim. When he was eleven, he wanted to swim faster, so he made wooden paddles that fit over his hands—almost like flippers! He did swim a lot faster, but his wrists got very tired from using the paddles.

Once Benjamin tied himself to a kite that pulled him across the water.

Benjamin the Apprentice

Because most families were large and needed money, kids in Benjamin's time went to work when they were very young. Many signed on to be an *apprentice* (uh-PREN-tis).

Apprentices worked for expert craftsmen to learn skills such as shoe or furniture making so they too could make a living. They signed contracts promising to work for a set number of years. Many promised to work until they turned twenty-one.

By the time he was ten, Benjamin had only been to school for two years. His father decided he needed to go to work and gave him a job at his soap and candle shop. Benjamin spent his days trimming candlewicks and running errands.

Benjamin didn't like this job. What he did like was reading. James, Benjamin's older brother, owned a printshop that printed books, newspapers, and articles. Josiah asked him to take Benjamin on as his apprentice.

Step 1: Setting up letters on paper

Step 3: Pulling a lever on the printer called <u>the devil's tail</u> that presses the ink into the paper

Ben signed a contract promising to work for James until he was twenty-one. The contract said he'd obey his brother and not get married, play cards, or drink alcohol. In exchange, James would pay for his food, some clothes, and a place to live.

Step 2: Inking paper with ink balls

Early printing press

Today printing presses use electricity, but in Benjamin's day people operated them by hand. Benjamin's main job was to set up the letters one by one on the printing press. He also trudged door-to-door selling a newspaper called *The New-England Courant*, which James published.

Letters were stored in a letter box like this.

Benjamin and His Books

Benjamin was happiest reading. Since there were no libraries in Boston and he didn't have money to buy books, he borrowed them from friends or read things from the shop.

Every night, Benjamin sat up late reading and studying. He became his own best teacher. By the time he was a teenager, he'd learned more math, better English grammar, some great writing skills, and much more.

Benjamin was interested in almost everything. Because he loved the sea, he read books on sailing. He even read a book urging people to stop eating meat. (He actually stopped for a short time.)

Mrs. Silence Dogood

When Benjamin was sixteen, he wanted to write for the newspaper. James was so jealous of him that he wouldn't allow it. Benjamin secretly began to write funny articles that made fun of people and things.

Benjamin didn't want anyone, especially his brother, to know that he was the writer, so he slipped his articles under the printshop door. He signed them as *Mrs. Silence Dogood*. People all over

town were curious about who Mrs. Dogood was. Ben pretended Mrs. Dogood was a widow. The newspaper got letters from men asking to marry her!

Apprentices were often harshly treated. Although Benjamin and James worked closely together, James had a bad temper and often hit or yelled at his brother.

It was against the law for apprentices to leave before their contract was up. In 1723, with several years left on his contract, Benjamin ran away from Boston.

A New Life

He packed a few clothes and took the small amount of money he'd made selling his books. Then Benjamin boarded a boat to New York City, where he hoped to find a job. Since there was no work for him in New York, he headed to Philadelphia, a city about a hundred miles away.

In order to get there, Ben walked fifty miles. Then he took a ship, and then he rowed a boat! It was a hard trip, and he felt sick. He'd read that drinking lots of cold water would make him feel better. He drank a lot!

Benjamin arrived dirty, hungry, and very tired. He went into a bakery and spent a precious few of his coins on three rolls. Then he strolled down the street eating one, with the other two tucked under each arm. Since Benjamin's pockets were stuffed with shirts and socks, he was quite a sight!

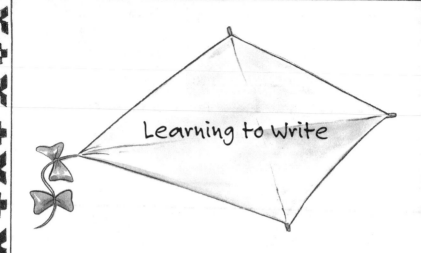

Learning to Write

At the printshop Benjamin often read articles in a journal called the *Spectator*. He tried to write the same articles from memory. After he finished writing, he'd read the *Spectator* again. If he didn't think what he'd written was good enough, he'd rewrite it over and over.

Benjamin became an excellent writer. Throughout his life he produced books and thousands of letters and articles. He sent or received over 15,000 letters in

28

his life! His most famous book is the story of his life.

2

Benjamin Franklin of Philadelphia

Benjamin spent his first night in Philadelphia in a rooming house. Without even taking off his clothes, he flopped down onto the bed and slept for hours. The next day, he went out to find a job.

Benjamin wandered into a dusty little printshop. Mr. Keimer, its owner, agreed to hire him. He also found a room to rent in a nearby house. The couple that owned the house had a daughter about Benjamin's age named Deborah Read. A few days earlier, Deborah had passed Benjamin on the street and laughed at the sight of this strange young man who looked so funny. Now he was living in her parents' house!

Deborah Read

Benjamin, England, and the Lying Governor

Benjamin began to make friends in Philadelphia. He even got to know Sir William Keith, the colony's English governor. A year after Ben arrived, he wanted to open his own printing shop. The best place to buy a press was in London, England.

Governor Keith promised he would send letters to people in London agreeing to pay any debts that Benjamin might owe after buying the press.

Benjamin traveled to England on a ship. After seven weeks of storms and rough seas, he finally landed. To his dismay, he found out that the governor had lied—he hadn't sent any letters at all!

Benjamin didn't have any money and badly needed a job. He found one at Samuel Palmer's printing house—a famous London printer. He spent some of his free time swimming in the River Thames (TEMZ), which runs through London. His swimming skills got so much attention that a rich man offered him a

Several years later Ben passed Governor Keith on the street, and the governor turned away in shame.

job teaching his children to swim. Benjamin had so many things he wanted to do that he didn't take the job.

His Own Printshop

After eighteen months in London, he returned to Philadelphia. For a short time, Benjamin went back to work at Keimer's printshop. But by the time he was twenty-three, he and a partner had borrowed enough money to buy Keimer's business. Benjamin's shop became one of the busiest and most successful printshops in the colonies.

Around this time Deborah Read, the daughter of Benjamin's first landlord, became his wife.

A Busy Life

Mr. Keimer had published a newspaper. It was not a success, and in 1729, Benjamin bought it from him and named it the *Pennsylvania Gazette*. He wrote many of the articles and often signed them with false names. Benjamin's newspaper became the most popular in the colonies.

Some of Benjamin's fake names were Martha Careful, Anthony Afterwit, Alice Addertongue, and Silence Dogood.

Benjamin also started a club for men called the Junto. They met every Friday evening to talk about business and share ideas, especially about how to make Philadelphia a better city.

Poor Richard's Almanack

In 1732, Benjamin began writing a booklet called *Poor Richard's Almanack*. He signed his name Poor Richard.

Today we spell *almanack* as <u>almanac</u>. It's a small book printed yearly with information about the coming year.

People read all kinds of interesting and useful things in it. There were weather predictions, sunrise and sunset times, and a calendar for the year. Benjamin also put in a lot of good household tips. He even gave recipes for making wine and getting sugar from beets.

The almanac was full of poems, jokes, and stories. Benjamin gave advice with little sayings called *aphorisms* (AFF-uh-rih-zumz). One of the most famous is "Early to bed and early to rise makes a man healthy, wealthy, and wise."

People loved his silly jokes and funny stories. The

Poor Richard, 1733.
AN
Almanack
For the Year of Christ
1733,

Being the First after LEAP YEAR:

And makes since the Creation	Years
By the Account of the Eastern *Greeks*	7241
By the Latin Church, when ☉ ent. ♈	6932
By the Computation of *W.W*	5742
By the *Roman* Chronology	5682
By the *Jewish* Rabbies	5494

Wherein is contained

The Lunations, Eclipses, Judgment of the Weather, Spring Tides, Planets Motions & mutual Aspects, Sun and Moon's Rising and Setting, Length of Days, Time of High Water, Fairs, Courts, and observable Days

Fitted to the Latitude of Forty Degrees, and a Meridian of Five Hours West from *London,* but may without sensible Error, serve all the adjacent Places, even from *Newfoundland* to *South-Carolina.*

By *RICHARD SAUNDERS*, Philom.

PHILADELPHIA:
Printed and sold by *B. FRANKLIN*, at the New Printing Office near the Market.

The Third Impression.

When James Franklin died, Ben gave James's wife 500 copies of <u>Poor Richard's Almanack</u> to sell for extra money.

almanac was so popular that for twenty-five years Ben printed up to 10,000 copies a year!

A Duty to Help

Benjamin believed that people had a duty to improve their lives and their cities. His ideas about how to make Philadelphia a better place actually changed lives then—and now.

Because everyone in Philadelphia used fireplaces and candles, the city's wooden buildings often caught on fire. There were no firefighters to fight the blazes.

Early Philadelphia firefighters were called the <u>bucket brigade</u>.

In 1736, Benjamin organized the city's first volunteer fire department. As its fire chief, he and other volunteers filled leather buckets with water and raced to put any fire out.

Benjamin the Postmaster

In 1737, Benjamin was appointed postmaster of Philadelphia. For a while, his

This famous portrait of Benjamin as fire chief was painted sixty years after he died.

printing shop was also the post office.

Sixteen years later, Benjamin got the job as deputy postmaster general

of America. He wanted faster mail service. To figure out the fastest routes, he spent much of the next year riding 1,600 miles over roads used by mail carriers. His work paid off, and carriers began to deliver the mail twice a week instead of just once.

Benjamin and the Streets

Benjamin then turned his attention to Philadelphia's streets. They were dirty and uneven. Benjamin came up with a plan to pave the streets and have them swept clean.

Benjamin also organized a group of night watchmen to patrol the streets and keep them safe.

At night, the streetlights were so dim that people couldn't see where they were going. Oil burning in the lights made them sooty and dark. Benjamin invented a new four-sided light that was brighter. There was a funnel in each light to draw out the smoke.

Remembering how he had yearned for books as a boy, he created the first public lending library in Philadelphia. When people paid to join it, they could take out the books they wanted without having to buy them.

He and a well-known doctor founded the first public hospital in the city.

First Citizen of Philadelphia

Because Benjamin did so much, people have called him the First Citizen of Philadelphia. In 1748, at the age of forty-two, Benjamin stopped working at his printing press.

His work, especially *Poor Richard's Almanack*, had made him rich enough

Benjamin began a school that became
the University of Pennsylvania.

to live comfortably. He wanted to spend
the rest of his life doing good things for
others and spend more time on scientific
research.

Ben's List of Virtues

When he was twenty, and later, when he wrote a book about his life, Ben made a list of virtues, or the best ways to live a good life. Here are some of them:

1. Be sincere: Don't lie or say what you don't think or mean.

2. Silence: Only talk when you have something worth saying, not something silly or unkind.

3. Frugality: Don't waste things or spend a lot of money on items you don't need; spend only to help yourself or others.

4. Cleanliness: Keep your clothes, your house, and yourself clean.

5. Temperance: Don't eat or drink too much.

6. Industry: Stay busy doing useful things.

3

Scientist and Inventor

In the 1700s, many people, including Benjamin, had a growing interest in science. In 1744, he and some friends founded a group called the American Philosophical Society. Many of his friends, including George Washington, were members.

Benjamin wanted people to share interesting things they'd learned. They wrote about math, farming, nature, maps, and chemistry.

Although people had started to make new discoveries about electricity, Benjamin was eager to find out more. He began experiments to help uncover the secrets of this mysterious force.

One big question he had was whether lightning was a form of electricity. He came up with a way to find out. It was a risky one . . . one that could kill him.

Ben, the Kite, and the Key

One day in June 1752, storm clouds darkened the sky in Philadelphia. Lightning flashed and thunder shook the ground. As everyone headed for shelter, Benjamin and his son, William, stood outside in the rain. Benjamin flew a kite made from a large silk handkerchief. It had a thin metal rod attached to its tip and a metal key tied to the end of a silk ribbon.

An electrical charge from the storm clouds traveled down the rod and into the key. Ben touched the key, and his finger tingled. He knew from other small experiments he'd made that this was caused by electricity.

Thanks to Benjamin, the world found out that lightning is a type of electricity. And thanks to the good research he did for his experiment, he didn't die! (Yay, Ben!)

Lightning Rods

Buildings can catch on fire if lightning strikes them. After his kite experiment, Benjamin invented a lightning rod as protection from lightning strikes.

Lightning rod

The rods were iron poles with pointed tips. People attached them to the top of their buildings. When lightning struck, the rods drew electricity safely down into the ground rather than into the houses . . . or into the people!

Benjamin called this new invention the *Franklin rod.*

Benjamin never made money from his inventions. He felt they were for everyone to use.

Open Your Windows!

Benjamin was interested in medicine and diseases. He had many friends who were doctors, and they wrote letters to one another about discoveries in medicine.

Benjamin helped start the first hospital in Philadelphia. Unlike most people of his time, he thought fresh air was good for people and that cold air did not cause bad colds. (He was right!)

Benjamin often slept with his windows wide open. He was so sure that fresh air was healthy, he

even sat in his window with no clothes on for thirty minutes or more every day for an "air bath."

Benjamin and the Sea

In his lifetime, Benjamin crossed the Atlantic Ocean eight times. During his trips, he often measured the water temperature. He also wrote about how weather affected the ocean. Benjamin made a map of a strong ocean current called the Gulf Stream. It flows from the Caribbean, through the Gulf of Mexico, and into the Atlantic Ocean. Franklin tracked it in the Atlantic Ocean.

Ben knew that the lower level of a ship might fill with water. If the water leaked into other parts of the ship, it could sink.

Ben designed a ship with separate water-tight compartments.

He also thought up ways to avoid icebergs and how to help people survive on a sinking ship. He even designed a bowl divided into sections that kept soup from spilling over the edge when the ship tilted!

In rough seas, soup that spilled out of the center bowl would get caught in one of the smaller hollows.

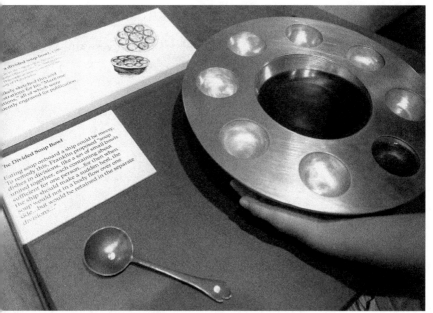

Franklin Stove

In the 1700s, everyone had fireplaces that burned wood. They used them for cooking and keeping warm in the winter. The problem was, their rooms were often smoky and there was always the danger of fire.

In 1741, Ben invented a wood-burning stove made of iron. People put it a few inches away from the back of their fireplace.

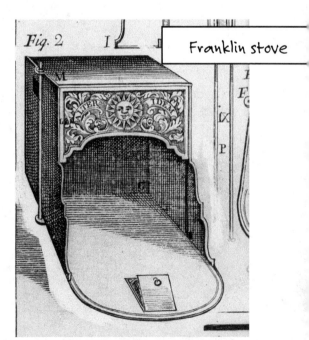

Franklin stove

Smoke escaped up the chimney through small holes in the bottom of the stove. When people used a Franklin stove, they needed much less wood.

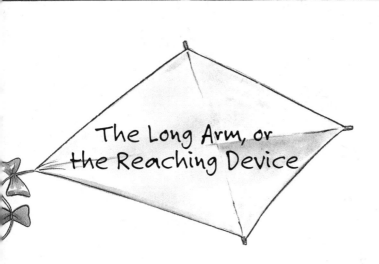

The Long Arm, or the Reaching Device

Ben had trouble reaching books on his highest bookshelves. Standing on a ladder made him dizzy.

He attached two thin pieces of wood to the top of an eight-foot pole. They looked like a thumb and finger on the end of a long arm. When Benjamin reached up for a book, he pulled a string, and the wooden fingers closed around the book so he could get it down.

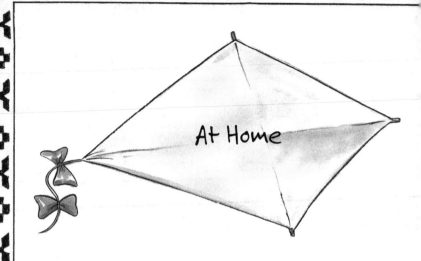

At Home

Ben also thought of ways to make life more comfortable at home.

He came up with a candle made from whale oil that gave off a good clear light. He invented a chair that he could turn into steps, and a chair that had a writing table arm on one side so he could write. Benjamin also put together a pulley

system that locked and unlocked his bedroom door so he could stay in bed.

Benjamin owned the first bathtub in the colonies! And since he liked to read in it, he invented a place on his bathtub for his books. But wait . . . he also invented the rocking chair!

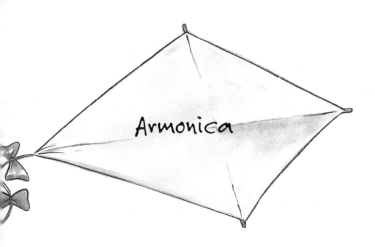

Armonica

Ben loved music and designed an instrument called a *glass armonica*. It was a line of glass bowls that turned as someone pushed a pedal.

People wet their fingers and rubbed them over the bowls. The armonica gave out such a pleasing musical sound that Mozart and Beethoven, two famous composers, wrote music for it. Ben said the glass armonica was his very favorite invention.

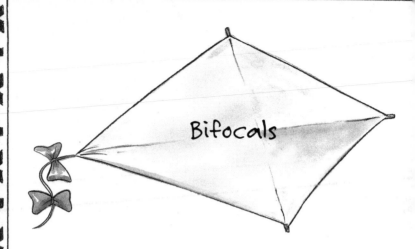

Bifocals

Benjamin needed one pair of glasses to see things up close and a second pair to see far away. He carried around two pairs of glasses to deal with this.

Trying to remember to bring two pairs of glasses was so annoying that in 1779, Benjamin decided to do something about it. He came up with a great idea. Why not put two different lenses together in one pair of glasses?

He had lenses in each set of glasses

cut in half. Then he had an optician join the two halves together into one frame. The top lens was for seeing far away, and the lower one was for reading close up. Benjamin had solved his problem! He called the new glasses double spectacles, but today we call them bifocals.

If you see glasses with a faint line running through the middle of the lenses, you're looking at bifocals!

4

Return to England

William Penn founded the colony of Pennsylvania in 1682. After he died, his three sons lived in England. They still owned most of the land in the colony. They were also in charge of the government.

While people in Pennsylvania had to pay taxes, the Penn brothers did not. The colonists felt this and other things the brothers did were unfair.

In 1757, the colonists hired Benjamin

to go to London. His job there was to end the Penn brothers' control of the colony. Benjamin and his son, William, boarded a ship bound for England.

One night a terrible storm woke everyone up. The ship was dangerously close to some rocks. Light from a nearby lighthouse showed the captain what was

ahead. (Ben strongly advised the colonies to build a lot of lighthouses!)

Benjamin and William in London

Because people in the colonies were English, Benjamin felt right at home in London. He was a city person at heart and enjoyed walking the crowded streets. He enjoyed meeting people in the coffee shops and taverns.

But Benjamin especially liked dinners with friends. These evenings were full of good talk, great food, and wine. Benjamin loved music and played the harp, guitar, and violin. He often went to concerts while he was in London.

Benjamin spent five years in London trying to work out problems with the Penn brothers. In spite of his efforts, the

English government would not agree to help the colonists. In 1762, Benjamin went back to Philadelphia.

The Stamp Act

Two years later, Benjamin was back on a ship bound for England. And once again he went to stand up for the interests of the colonists.

Stamp for court papers

Colonists had to pay to have their newspapers and documents stamped to show they'd paid their taxes. Things got serious when England demanded higher taxes on their stamps and sugar.

Pamphlet or newspaper stamp

68

The colonists were angry because they did not have a say in the matter. Mobs in Boston smashed the houses of a stamp officer and the lieutenant governor.

Many people believed that Benjamin supported the English. Deborah Franklin had remained in Philadelphia. When rioters marched to her house, a group of men called the White Oak Boys supported

Ben and defended his home. The mob turned back, and the night ended peacefully.

Franklin of Philadelphia

In spite of what the colonists thought, Benjamin had worked hard to get rid of the Stamp Act. In February 1766, he spoke in front of English lawmakers in the House of Commons. He rose to face them, and when they asked his name, he said, "Franklin, of Philadelphia."

The House of Commons in London is where English lawmakers meet.

Benjamin answered 174 questions, including many about how the act would affect the colonists. A week later the tax was canceled.

When colonists in Philadelphia heard, they cheered, rang bells, and burned bonfires. Three hundred people in the

Pennsylvania State House stood to toast Benjamin Franklin as their hero.

The Trouble Begins

Ben worked to represent not just Pennsylvania, but also Georgia, New Jersey, and Massachusetts.

For seven years following his Stamp Tax victory, he worked hard for the interests of the colonists. He wrote articles and held meetings. But England continued to tax the colonists without their consent. In 1773, the English still demanded a tax on tea. The colonists were very angry and decided to act.

The colonists drank tea more often than they drank coffee.

Boston Tea Party

In December 1773, a group of men calling themselves the Sons of Liberty dressed in a Native American style as a disguise. Then they gathered at Boston's harbor, where a ship loaded with tea was docked. They leapt on board and broke open 342 chests of tea with their tomahawks. Then they threw the chests into the water.

It took three hours for them to destroy a fortune in tea!

This was the colonists' first serious protest against English rule. The English were outraged. They took their anger out on Benjamin Franklin. He was called before a government council. Ben-

jamin listened quietly for an hour as an English lawyer accused him of being a thief and a liar.

In 1774, the British closed the port of Boston and removed Benjamin from his job. They also sent more soldiers to America to keep order.

Fearing that the English would arrest him if he stayed, on March 20, 1775, Benjamin sailed home. His return trip took nearly two months.

This same year, Benjamin's wife, Deborah, died.

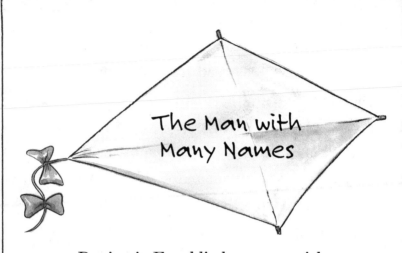

The Man with
Many Names

Benjamin Franklin has many nicknames. Because of all the work he did for the colonies and the United States, he is sometimes called the First American. This nickname was given to him after he died.

However, some nicknames were given to him during his life. When he was in England, most of the workers at the printer's drank beer. Benjamin always drank water, so people called him Water-American.

Some names Benjamin gave himself. Writers in Benjamin's days often used fake names to sign their work. Benjamin used many different names! Silence Dogood is probably his most famous, but here are some others:

Timothy Turnstone

lia Shortface

Martha Careful

ry Meanwell

Anthony Afterwit

Polly Baker

Busy Body

Richard Saunders

5

Ben and the Revolution

While Benjamin was still in England, the colonists signed a document saying that they wanted the freedom to make their own rules. People began to form *militias* and prepare to fight the English.

Militias are groups of people who are not part of a regular army but are ready to fight if needed.

The English refused to honor the colonists' demands. Instead they ordered their soldiers in America to take the colonists' weapons and arrest some of their leaders.

On April 19, 1775, the first battles of the Revolutionary War began in the villages of Lexington and Concord, Massachusetts. Seven hundred English soldiers marched to Lexington to destroy weapons and powder that the colonists had there.

Some American militiamen were called minutemen, because they could fight at a moment's notice.

Seventy-seven minutemen met them there in a fight that lasted only a few minutes. Eight of them died, and nine were injured. One British soldier was injured. On the way back to Boston, the British marched through the village of Concord.

When word of this spread, 400 minutemen grabbed their muskets and raced to Concord. They attacked the soldiers, killing 250 of them and only losing 90 of their own men. The next day, the British raided buildings where the colonists kept weapons and gunpowder.

Benjamin Returns Home to War

Benjamin came home two weeks after the Battles of Lexington and Concord. He strongly believed that the colonists should be free from England.

Beginning in May 1775, *delegates* from all the colonies met to plan for war with England. Their meetings took place in Philadelphia and were named the Second Continental Congress.

Delegates are people chosen to speak and act for others.

Pennsylvania sent Benjamin as one of its delegates. The congress elected George Washington as commander of the army.

At sixty-nine, Ben was not as young as the other men in the congress. But he was busy for the next year and a half and served on many committees.

George Washington

Thomas Jefferson, a young delegate from Virginia, said that when George Washington and Benjamin Franklin spoke, they never spoke for more than ten minutes, and every single thing they said was important.

Ben Gets Super Busy

Ben worked hard to get gunpowder and lead for bullets. He also became postmaster general again. He helped to make

mail service faster so people could get
news about the war.

In the fall of 1775, Ben and two other committee members met with General George Washington at his camp near Boston. They planned ways to improve the army and get supplies to the troops faster.

The next spring Benjamin traveled to Canada by boat in a snowstorm. His plan was to get help for the Americans from the colonists in Canada. After his boat ride, Benjamin headed to the city of Montreal. The roads were rough and bumpy. Each night he slept outside in the woods, hungry and cold. When Benjamin arrived in Montreal he was a wreck—his skin covered in boils, his legs swollen.

Although he tried hard to win the Canadians over, very few agreed to help. Ben returned home with a heavy heart, worried that the soldiers might starve and have to surrender.

The Declaration of Independence

In June 1776, a committee met in Philadelphia to write the Declaration of Independence. The Declaration was going to say that America was to be a nation free from English rule. From now on the colonies would be called the United States of America.

This was a daring and dangerous thing to do. The English would think of this as a crime and could order all the rebels to be hanged.

Thomas Jefferson wrote most of the Declaration. Benjamin stepped in and made some of the words simpler and clearer.

On July 8, 1776, bells rang out all over Philadelphia to call people to meet at Independence Hall. The crowd listened quietly as Colonel John Nixon read the Declaration of Independence.

Immediately afterward, bells rang again all over the city. They chimed

John Trumbull's famous painting <u>Declaration of Independence</u> now hangs in the U.S. Capitol.

throughout the day. People tore down the British royal coat of arms from the state house and burned it.

Benjamin Goes to France

The colonies had little money to spend on the war. The English had well-trained soldiers with plenty of weapons. Their navy was one of the best in the world. Americans didn't have any of these things. There were no large factories that made weapons, no navy, and few trained soldiers.

Farmers, shopkeepers, and tradesmen from all the colonies joined the militia. Many of them were young and eager to fight. The soldiers often went without enough clothing, weapons, and food. Yet George Washington always managed to give them courage and hope.

In the fall of 1776, British soldiers captured New York City. With their army of 32,000 soldiers, they outnumbered George Washington's small army by two to one.

The Americans badly needed help from other countries. They sent Benjamin to France to try to get some aid. He

took his young grandsons, Temple and Benny, along with him and boarded a ship for France.

The voyage was hard, with poor food and bad weather. Benjamin was sick in his cabin most of the time, but every day he went up on the deck to take temperature readings of the Gulf Stream.

Benjamin Arrives in Paris

The French stared at this old man who looked so different in his fur hat and simple brown suit. When Ben walked down the street, he carried a walking stick made from a crab apple tree.

The French were used to important people dressing in powdered wigs and silk clothes. But now everyone wanted to

Benjamin felt his simple clothes made him look more American.

meet the plainly dressed visitor from the colonies.

Benjamin was already famous as a scientist. He made friends with French scientists and writers. He was so popular that artists painted his portrait, and his

Ben and his French friends often played chess. In 1999, he was voted into the U.S. Chess Hall of Fame.

face appeared on many objects like cups, watches, and rings. People often invited Benjamin to parties. He enjoyed telling amusing stories and flirting with the ladies. Women styled their hair to look like Benjamin's hats. They also wore hats with metal rods sticking out of them that looked like lightning rods. Men carried lightning rod umbrellas.

Lightning rod umbrella

Lightning rod hat

Benjamin Gets Help

France and England had often been at war. This is why the American colonists thought that the French would support their fight against the English.

Ben lived in France for nine years.

Ben knew that the French would help only if they believed America had a chance to win. He kept bad news about the war from his French friends.

In 1777, the Americans won the Battle of Saratoga in New York and captured 5,000 British soldiers. General Washington and his men began to feel hopeful of a victory.

This was the first time the Americans had won a major battle.

Benjamin and the King

In February 1778, the French signed a treaty with the patriots. It proclaimed that France was on America's side.

91

In March, the king of France invited Ben to his palace. The old man arrived in a plain brown suit with glasses perched on his nose. His hair was long, and he carried a hat under one arm.

People were worried that the king would be shocked at Benjamin's simple clothes. But he greeted him warmly. The king promised to send money to the colonies. And throughout the war, France sent millions of dollars.

The Marquis (mar-KEE) de Lafayette, who was a famous French soldier, sailed to America to fight with the colonists. He commanded several battles and got supplies to the soldiers.

The French navy also helped the colonists by stopping English supply ships heading to the colonies.

Lafayette

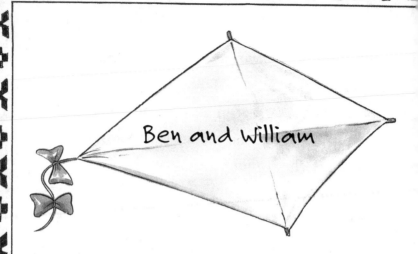

Ben and William

Not all colonists wanted freedom from English rule. Many were loyal to England and felt America had no chance of winning.

When he was young, William Franklin had lived in England and knew the country well. When the war began, he was governor of the colony of New Jersey. William sided with the British. He sent information about the patriots to London and urged his father to remain loyal to the king.

Benjamin was heartbroken. He felt

betrayed and broke off all contact with his son. Because of his actions, William was sent to prison for helping the enemy. In 1782, he returned to England, where he spent the rest of his life. Ben and William were never close again, and they would see each other only once more.

6

Final Years

The war ended on October 17, 1781, when George Washington defeated General Cornwallis's army at the Battle of Yorktown in Virginia. As the British surrendered, French soldiers in their neat blue and white uniforms stood side by side with the ragged American army.

The war had lasted for seven years. Now that the fighting was over, America was free. Benjamin and some other Americans went to Paris to draw up a peace treaty with England. In 1783, Ben and two other Americans signed the Treaty of Paris.

Benjamin Goes Home

In 1785, after many parties, honors, and celebrations, Ben sailed home. Even though he was seventy-nine, he was still active and ready to jump back into life in America.

Ben lived with his daughter, Sarah "Sally" Bache, and his grandchildren. He spent a lot of time enjoying life and visiting with his old friends. George Washington even stopped by for a chat!

America in Crisis

Two years after its victory, America was still struggling. The biggest problem was that the government was not strong enough to govern all the states well. There was no way to collect taxes or make laws.

On May 25, 1787, fifty-five men from all the states except Rhode Island met in Independence Hall in Philadelphia. They were there to hold a Constitutional Convention. Their goal was to form a single

Abraham Lincoln visited the same room where the U.S. Constitution and the Declaration of Independence were signed.

government that could make laws for all the states.

Guards stood at the doors, and windows were kept shut so nobody could hear what the delegates were saying.

At the age of eighty-one, Ben was the oldest delegate. His friend George Washington was chosen as president of the convention.

Independence Hall served as the Pennsylvania State House.

For four months they worked hard writing the United States Constitution. It laid out the way the government should work and laws that Americans should obey.

Benjamin was carried to the meetings in a sedan chair. Every time he entered the hall, the delegates stood as a sign of respect.

The Constitutional Convention was Benjamin's final duty. But there was one last thing he wanted to do. Benjamin urged Congress to end slavery. He became head of the Pennsylvania *Abolition* Society and argued that all people deserve to be free.

Abolition means putting an end to something.

Benjamin had been sick for a while, and on April 17, 1790, he died. He was eighty-four years old. Two of his

Delegates finally signed the Constitution on September 17, 1787.

grandsons and his daughter were at his bedside.

In his will, Benjamin left money to the

Temple didn't take good care of Benjamin's papers, and many were lost.

People in France also mourned his passing.

cities of Boston and Philadelphia to help young tradesmen who had been apprentices. George Washington got his favorite walking stick, and his grandson Temple received Ben's library and papers.

On April 21, 1790, a crowd of 20,000 people gathered for Ben's funeral. Since only 28,000 people lived in Philadelphia, his was the largest funeral the city had ever seen. Ships in the harbor lowered their flags to half-mast. Scientists, doctors, members of the American

Philosophical Society, and printers walked in the procession with his casket.

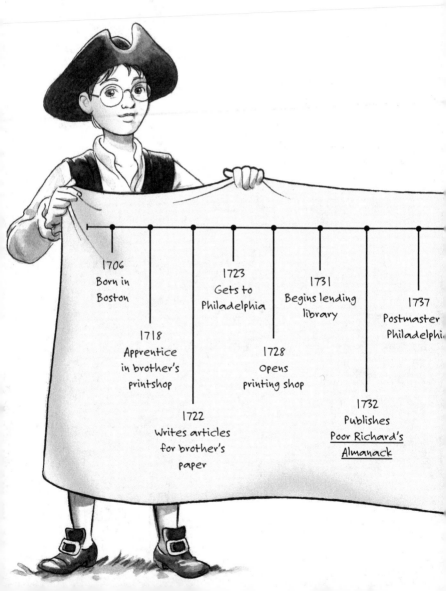

1706
Born in
Boston

1718
Apprentice
in brother's
printshop

1722
Writes articles
for brother's
paper

1723
Gets to
Philadelphia

1728
Opens
printing shop

1731
Begins lending
library

1732
Publishes
Poor Richard's
Almanack

1737
Postmaster
Philadelphi

Benjamin was buried next to his wife
and a son who had died when he was four.

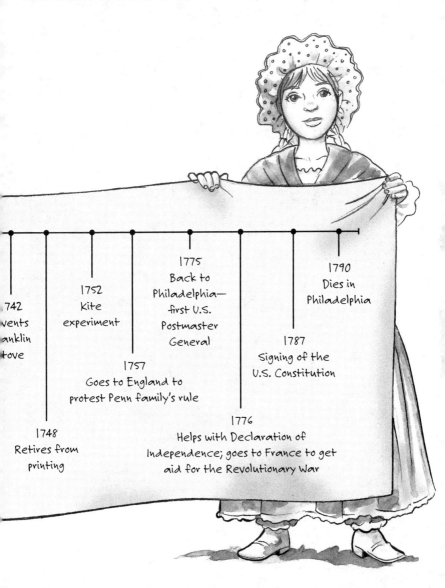

742
vents
anklin
tove

1748
Retires from
printing

1752
Kite
experiment

1757
Goes to England to
protest Penn family's rule

1775
Back to
Philadelphia—
first U.S.
Postmaster
General

1776
Helps with Declaration of
Independence; goes to France to get
aid for the Revolutionary War

1787
Signing of the
U.S. Constitution

1790
Dies in
Philadelphia

7

Founding Father

Men like Ben Franklin, Thomas Jefferson, and George Washington risked everything they had, including their lives, for their country. If America had lost, they would have been put to death for fighting against the king. They are heroes who formed our young country and made it what it is today. These men were among the people known as our Founding Fathers.

Benjamin was the only one who signed all four great documents of the revolution. They were the Declaration of Independence, the Treaty of Alliance with France, the Treaty of Paris, and the Constitution. His face is on the $100 bill because he was so important to our history.

There are only two non-presidents with their faces on our bills—Benjamin Franklin and a patriot named Alexander Hamilton.

All He Did

Benjamin lived so many lives in just one lifetime. He was a printer, writer, publisher, merchant, inventor, scientist, educator, statesman, postmaster general, and peacemaker.

Ben was wise when his young country needed wisdom and brave when it needed bravery. Most of all he was curious. Everything interested him, including science, crops, trees, business, birds, animals, the climate, and beekeeping!

Ben strongly believed that people could improve themselves by learning and doing good things. His well-lived life was proof that everything he believed is absolutely true. Thomas Jefferson was right when he said that no one could ever replace this great man.

Doing More Research

There's a lot more you can learn about Benjamin Franklin. The fun of research is seeing how many different sources you can explore.

Books

Most libraries and bookstores have books about Benjamin Franklin.

Here are some things to remember when you're using books for research:

1. You don't have to read the whole book. Check the table of contents and the index to find the topics you're interested in.

2. Write down the name of the book.

When you take notes, make sure you write down the name of the book in your notebook so you can find it again.

3. Never copy exactly from a book.

When you learn something new from a book, put it in your own words.

4. Make sure the book is <u>nonfiction</u>.

Some books tell make-believe stories about Benjamin Franklin. Make-believe stories are called *fiction*. They're fun to read, but not good for research.

Research books have facts and tell true stories. They are called *nonfiction*. A librarian or teacher can help you make sure the books you use for research are nonfiction.

Here are some good nonfiction books
about Benjamin Franklin:

- *The Amazing Life of Benjamin Franklin*
  by James Cross Giblin
- *Ben Franklin: A Man of Many Talents*
  by the Editors of *TIME for Kids* with
  Kathryn Hoffman Satterfield
- *Benjamin Franklin: A Man with
  Many Jobs*, Rookie Biography series,
  by Carol Greene
- *Benjamin Franklin: A Photographic
  Story of a Life*, DK Biography series,
  by Stephen Krensky
- *Benjamin Franklin: Young Printer*,
  Childhood of Famous Americans series,
  by Augusta Stevenson
- *Who Was Ben Franklin?*
  by Dennis Brindell Fradin

Museums

Many museums can help you learn more about Benjamin Franklin.

When you go to a museum:

1. Be sure to take your notebook!
Write down anything that catches your interest. Draw pictures, too!

2. Ask questions.
There are almost always people at museums who can help you find what you're looking for.

3. Check the calendar.
Many museums have special events and activities just for kids!

Here are some museums where you can learn about Benjamin Franklin:

- Benjamin Franklin Museum (Philadelphia)

- Boston Tea Party Ships and Museum (Boston)

- The Franklin Institute Science Museum (Philadelphia)

- Independence Hall (Philadelphia)

- Museum of the American Revolution (Philadelphia)

- National Archives Museum (Washington, D.C.)

Internet

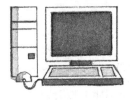

Many websites have lots of facts about Benjamin Franklin. Some also have activities that can help make learning about Benjamin Franklin easier.

Ask your teacher or your parents to help you find more websites like these:

- ducksters.com/biography /ben_franklin.php
- enchantedlearning.com/inventors /page/f/franklin.shtml
- factsforkids.net/benjamin-franklin-facts -for-kids-first-american
- fi.edu/benjamin-franklin-faq

- kids.britannica.com/kids/article/Benjamin-Franklin/353147

- kidsdiscover.com/shop/issues/ben-franklin-for-kids

- socialstudiesforkids.com/articles/ushistory/benjaminfranklininventions.htm

- ushistory.org/franklin/info

Bibliography

Brands, H. W. *The First American: The Life and Times of Benjamin Franklin.* New York: Doubleday, 2000.

Encyclopaedia Britannica. *The Founding Fathers: The Essential Guide to the Men Who Made America.* Hoboken: John Wiley & Sons, Inc., 2007.

Franklin, Benjamin. *The Autobiography of Benjamin Franklin.* Boston: Houghton Mifflin Company, 1928.

Franklin, Benjamin. *Poor Richard's Almanack.* Waterloo: The U.S.C. Publishing Co., 1914.

Isaacson, Walter. *Benjamin Franklin: An American Life.* New York: Simon & Schuster, 2003.

Morgan, Edmund S. *Benjamin Franklin.* New Haven: Yale University Press, 2002.

Schiff, Stacy. *A Great Improvisation: Franklin, France, and the Birth of America.* New York: Henry Holt and Company, 2005.

Index

*Have you read the adventure that
matches up with this book?*

Don't miss
Magic Tree House® #32

To the Future, Ben Franklin!

The magic tree house whisks Jack and
Annie back in time to meet Ben Franklin.
The famously curious Founding Father
and inventor is intrigued by them
and their tree house.

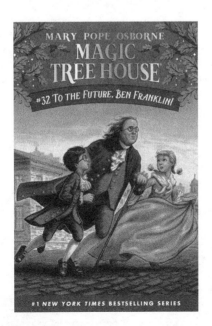

Magic Tree House®

Magic Tree House®
Merlin Missions

Magic Tree House®
Super Edition

Magic Tree House®
Fact Trackers

More Magic Tree House®

A WORLD OF MAGICAL READING ADVENTURES AWAITS YOUR CHILD!

Dragons, Pirates, Dinosaurs . . . Hawaii, Houdini, and More!

MAGIC TREE HOUSE®

KIDS'
ADVENTURE CLUB
IS NOW ONLINE

THERE'S SO MUCH TO DO:

Kids can track their reading progress,
collect passport stamps, earn rewards, join
reading challenges to unlock special prizes,
and travel the world with Jack and Annie.

Visit MagicTreeHouse.com
to register your child for the
Kids' Adventure Club!